THE STORY OF

MINI

Published in 2021 by Welbeck

An Imprint of Welbeck Non-Fiction Limited, part of Welbeck Publishing Group.

20 Mortimer Street London W1T 3JW

Text © Welbeck Non-Fiction Limited, part of Welbeck Publishing Group.

All rights reserved. No part of this publication may be reproduced, stored in a retrieval
system, or transmitted in any form or by any means, electronically, mechanical,
photocopying, recording or otherwise, without the prior permission of the copyright
owners and the publishers.

A CIP catalogue record for this book is available from the British Library

ISBN 9781787399266

Editor: Ross Hamilton
Design: Eliana Holder & Luana Gobbo
Picture Research: Paul Langan
Production: Arlene Alexander

Printed in Dubai

10 9 8 7 6 5 4 3 2 1

Disclaimer:
All trademarks, images, quotations, company names, registered names, products, logos
used or cited in this book are the property of their respective owners and are used in this
book for identification, review and editorial purposes only. This book is a publication
of Welbeck Non-Fiction Limited and has not been licensed, approved, sponsored, or
endorsed by any person or entity and has no connection or association to BMW (UK)
Holdings Limited and BMW AG owner of MINI)

THE STORY OF
MINI

A CELEBRATION
OF THE ICONIC CAR

BEN CUSTARD

WELBECK

CONTENTS

A 60-YEAR STORY

BRITAIN, BEATLES AND BMW

It's often said that the best things come in small packages
– and, in terms of cars, things don't get much smaller than
the classic Mini. Measuring just three metres (nearly 10ft)
long, the Mini was dwarfed by most of the cars it was on sale
against and it feels even smaller now, as cars continue to grow
and high-riding SUVs become increasingly popular.

However, a car doesn't rack up over five million sales worldwide
just because it's a tiny, novelty machine. Despite being so
compact, the Mini could seat four people, take at least some of
their luggage and entertain everyone on board while doing so.
There are plenty of bigger cars that can't manage these things,
because the space inside isn't used so efficiently. The Mini is a
masterclass in packaging, and pretty much set the template for
a generation of small "economy" cars that followed.

Other manufacturers had plenty of time to check out the
Mini and take inspiration from it, as it enjoyed one of the
longest production runs in history. Cars are often replaced after
a decade or so in European countries, but the Mini stayed in

OPPOSITE: The Mini was built to take on microcars like the
Messerschmitt bubble car. Another small car from the '50s, the Fiat 500,
reached similarly iconic status.

ABOVE: Mini trio Arguably its most iconic movie role, three Minis were used in the 1969 film *The Italian Job*.

continuous production for over 40 years. The original 1959 design was, more or less, still being sold in the year 2000.

The makers of the Mini couldn't have expected such success, and at the very start sales of the car were slow. But the Mini caught the eyes of countless celebrities, and quickly became a central part of 1960s British culture. Sir Paul McCartney had one – a very swanky one, at that – and so did all of his Beatles bandmates. Actors and models such as Peter Sellers and Twiggy both enjoyed Minis, as did many members of the public, who liked the idea of driving the same car as their heroes.

The Mini's iconic status was further increased thanks to a number of film and TV appearances, in which it would often be the hero itself. Its most famous role came in the 1969 film *The Italian Job*, where three Minis were used as getaway cars for a bank heist – and they were integral to the film. There were special-edition versions of the Mini marketed off the back of the film, and a remake using three of the new MINI hatchbacks when it launched at the start of the twenty-first century.

Alternatively, you might immediately recognize the Mini from its starring role in the television comedy show *Mr Bean*, in which it's the vehicle of choice for Rowan Atkinson's well-known bumbling character. You could say it's as unique as the character himself, with bright green paint and a black bonnet, plus a key and padlock and the option to steer it from an armchair mounted on the roof!

Like *Mr Bean*, the Mini was a worldwide export – right from the start. It was launched in almost one hundred countries globally, and found buyers in nearly every corner of the world, including Japan, Australia and South America. That's perhaps not surprising when you consider that the Mini was made in a number of factories; most were built in Longbridge, in Birmingham, but examples were also manufactured in Portugal, Chile and even New Zealand.

The Mini sometimes went by other names in different countries – such as the Austin 850 in France and the Morris Mascot in Denmark – and even in the UK you could buy Minis with different badges. When it was launched in 1959, the Mini was sold as the Morris Mini Minor and the Austin Seven. Everything about the two cars was identical, apart from the wheel caps, grille and the paint colours you could choose. The Mini design came with plenty of different badges and names throughout its production; various ownership changes throughout its life meant that it was seemingly re-badged every few years. That's probably why most people simply refer to the car as "the Mini", as we're doing here.

You could also choose from estate, van and even pickup versions of the Mini, but its influence didn't stop there. The Mini's underpinnings would go on to be used for all sorts of aftermarket models and kit cars, where a different body style

LEFT: The Austin Seven Countryman was one of the first Mini spin-offs – an estate take on the compact car that featured a pair of rear 'barn doors' for easy access.

OPPOSITE: Minis rounded out the top three at the 1966 Monte Carlo rally, but all three were controversially disqualified.

OVERLEAF: The Mini's cheery face is instantly recognizable thanks to its round headlights and chromed grille.

could be put on the top. Many of these would be sports cars, which benefited from the Mini's agile handling and low weight. A jeep-like model was even produced with a military application in mind, and that in turn led to the Mini Moke buggy, which found its place in sunny coastal parts of America and Australia.

While it was sold and adapted worldwide, the Mini was always a symbol of Britishness – and indeed that's a large part of why it found success. It was revered in Japan for its charming retro looks, and probably featured in the same stereotypes as cups of tea, cheery butlers and bowler hats.

The Mini sits alongside other hugely successful small cars of the twentieth century such as the Fiat 500 and Volkswagen Beetle, but one thing sets it apart. While it might not look like an obvious contender at first glance, the Mini quickly became known for its appearances and wins in various forms of motorsport. It is particularly associated with the Monte Carlo Rally, as Minis won the time trial around the hills above Monaco three times in the 1960s – and another win was later disqualified. Many racing drivers who are now household names started in a Mini, and some would go on to win the Formula 1 World Championship. These include Sir Jackie Stewart and the late Niki Lauda.

Its motorsport pedigree no doubt increased sales and helped the Mini live on for as long as it did. But as the car entered the 1980s and 1990s, it was becoming increasingly outmoded and long in the tooth. Buyers who needed a car that was cheap to run and easy to park still flocked to the Mini – and it was a popular first car to own – but many customers were drawn towards the Austin Metro, which made its debut in 1980. It was bigger and more spacious than the Mini, and gave British Leyland a model to compete with the Ford Fiesta and Volkswagen Polo, which were both introduced in the late 1970s.

1984 marked the 25th anniversary of the Mini, so a limited edition was launched to celebrate the occasion. Special editions became a regular part of the Mini range, all with restricted production runs and unique combinations of colour and trim. Many were named after London boroughs, and others focused on a specific paint shade. These models helped to keep the Mini fresh and appealing until it was eventually phased out in October 2000. By the 1990s, the Mini was regarded as a retro icon, a symbol of nostalgia from the car's heyday.

BMW had bought the Rover Group (the company making the Mini in the '90s, which had previously been part of British Leyland) in 1994, and let Rover still sell the classic Mini while it pondered how to create a successor. A couple of zany-looking concepts were revealed in 1997, as a build-up to the new MINI, and the car eventually went on sale in July 2001.

ABOVE: The interior of the classic Mini was minimalist, and a handy shelf was created where the dashboard would normally be found in other cars.

The new MINI was a clean-sheet design, although it borrowed many of the styling details from its predecessor. A rounded grille, circular headlights, windscreens that were nearly upright and a slightly domed roof were all included to give a similar appearance to the classic model. It was a near-instant sales success, although it was often criticized for being too big – but that was necessary to fit modern safety features and allow more space. You would hear jokes like "it should have been called the Maxi!" and lots of sour remarks from classic Mini lovers. One stinger came from Dr Alex Moulton, who had designed the rubber cone suspension of the original 1959 car, and clearly wasn't a fan of all the new safety equipment.

"It's enormous. The Mini was the best-packaged car of all time; this [new one] is an example of how not to do it. The interior space is not much bigger than the old Mini,

BELOW: By contrast, the contemporary MINI interiors are crafted with style, elegance and comfort in mind.

but it's huge on the outside and weighs the same as the Austin Maxi!

"The crash protection has been taken too far. I mean, what do you want… an armoured car? Princess Diana was killed in a two-tonne Mercedes: you can have a fatal accident in anything if you drive fast enough.

"To be honest, it's an irrelevance in so far that it has no part in the Mini story."

BMW's ownership took the MINI upmarket, and it was arguably the first premium supermini – something a bit more luxurious than a Ford Fiesta or a Renault Clio. It's always had an emphasis on sportiness and being fun to drive as well, although that comes at the cost of comfort on some models – especially the hardcore John Cooper Works versions, which are the fastest incarnations of the modern MINI and are set up to be quick on a race track.

OPPOSITE: The Mini was a very fashionable car, so it was often seen in very prestigious locations.

BELOW: Past and present, side by side – the original Mini and a modern MINI.

OPPOSITE:
Personalization has
always been a key
aspect of the Mini
– and you can make
yours individual with
various styling packs.

The German car maker saw money-making potential with the MINI brand, not only with a re-imagination of the classic car but with a number of new models as well. Soon, a MINI Convertible hit the road, as did a Clubman estate with barn doors and an extra door on the right-hand side to gain access to the rear seats. A Countryman crossover was introduced to take on 2007's Nissan Qashqai, which seemed to be the car of the moment for many new car buyers. But sometimes the range was stretched a bit too far, as was the case with the two-seat MINI Coupe and the MINI Paceman, a three-door lowered version of the Countryman. Both were quietly withdrawn after only a couple of years on sale.

Diesel engined-models made up a good proportion of sales a few years ago, but now these engines have been all but phased out of the MINI range. In fact, MINI has confirmed that all its engines will soon be discontinued, as the brand will only sell electric cars by 2030. That's the year that the UK government plans to ban sales of new petrol and diesel cars. One MINI EV (electric vehicle) is available at the time of writing, a version of the hatchback, plus a plug-in hybrid version of the Countryman.

Whichever Mini you drive, whether classic or modern, there are thousands of like-minded owners out there. There are also knowledgeable owners' groups if you encounter a problem or want to share your ride, and companies set up specifically to provide Mini parts – both for restoring classic models and adding a personal touch with aftermarket modifications. The Mini's popularity has enabled a feeling of community amongst fans and owners.

But how did the Mini's remarkable success come about? Read on to find out.

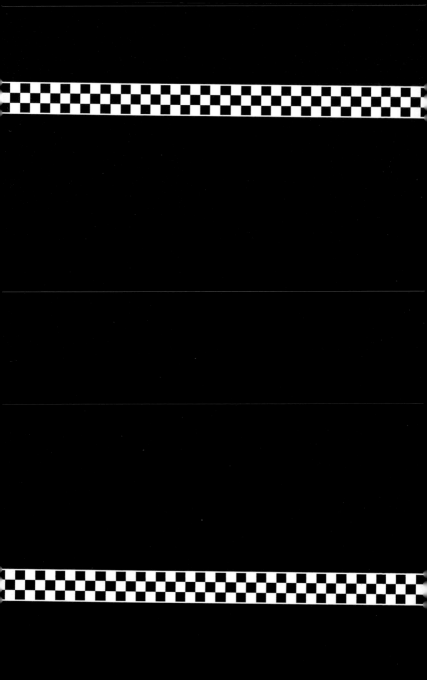

THE MAKING
OF THE MINI

ONE MAN'S MINI VISION

Nowadays, a car is designed by a whole committee of people, whose job it is to argue about nearly every aspect of the vehicle. Before a car reaches production, every line, button, feature and trim name will have been scrutinized – often in glossy design studios with adventure-themed mood boards – just in case someone does actually take their 4x4 off-road.

However, this most certainly was not the case with the Mini, which was designed primarily by one man: Sir Alec Issigonis. He was re-hired to the British Motor Corporation (BMC) in 1955 after designing the Morris Minor, partly to design an even smaller car. The brief, given to him by BMC boss Leonard Lord, was fairly simple; the car must be three metres (nearly 10ft) long or less, and four-fifths of that should be passenger space. Four adults should be able to sit in the car, and the engine should already be in production – in order to reduce costs. Finally, the car had to be in production within just two years, which would be a challenge for an established manufacturer, even today.

OPPOSITE: Englishman Sir Alec Issigonis was given the task of designing the Mini. He'd previously designed the Morris Minor.

The 1950s in Britain wasn't the same as how the decade was often portrayed by Hollywood. Britain was still getting back on its feet after the Second World War, and the threat of a Cold War was looming, too. Petrol became freely available again in May 1950, having been severely rationed and of very low quality for the five years prior, but cars were often still much more expensive than they had been pre-war.

Later during the decade, in the Middle East, tensions rose over the Suez Canal, which was used to transport oil to European countries. In October 1956 the Suez War started; Egypt had blocked the canal, and the reintroduction of British troops probably hindered more than it helped. Oil – required for petrol and many other purposes – had to be transported all the way around the southern tip of Africa, so petrol was rationed again and private motorists were limited to around 300 miles of driving a month. Not only did Britain have very little petrol, it didn't have much money either – and the price of a lot of goods rose due to inflation.

Motorists clearly felt the squeeze, and many resorted to microcars – repeating a pattern that had begun after the First World War. Microcars – or "bubble" cars, as they were known – generally used tiny, noisy motorcycle engines with only one or two cylinders. They were light and very economical, so the petrol went further, but most struggled to reach 80kmh (50mph). All were ultimately flawed and looked very unusual. The BMW Isetta (made by an Italian refrigerator company) had only one door – mounted on the front end of the car – and no reverse gear. Many models had only three wheels, like the 197cc Scootacar or the Messerschmitt, which took its inspiration from aeroplanes. Not that you could tell from its wing-like wheel arches, a yoke in place of a steering wheel, or the side-opening canopy....

BMC president Leonard Lord hated all these microcars with a passion, and wanted a proper small car to replace them. Alec

Issigonis is believed to have sketched the original Mini design on a tablecloth, and drew a Mini-sized chalk rectangle around four chairs. He picked BMC's four-cylinder engine, which had already been used in the Morris Minor and the Austin Healey "Frogeye" Sprite. Mounted in the normal, longitudinal fashion, it would have been too long to fit the car, so Issigonis worked on mounting it sideways (transverse) in the engine bay. There was no room for the gearbox, so a masterful bit of Issigonis design saw it mounted beneath the engine, using the oil from the sump.

ABOVE: The Mini was created to get rid of bubble cars such as the BMW Isetta, which only had one door - that was mounted on the front end.

RIGHT: One of the bubble cars the Mini was up against – the Messerschmitt KR200 – clearly took its inspiration from aviation.

MAKERS OF THE MINI: SIR ALEC ISSIGONIS

Sir Alec Issigonis is regarded as the father of the Mini, with good reason – he designed pretty much the whole thing. He was born in 1906, to a Greek father with British nationality and a German mother, in what is now Izmir, on the western edge of Turkey. The family enjoyed a comfortable life until the outbreak of World War I – and trouble then continued for them after the war. Izmir became a part of Greece, and was invaded by Turkey in 1922. After a spell in a refugee camp in Malta, Alec and his mother travelled to England. His father became very ill and didn't survive the journey.

Alec had always been good at drawing and studied engineering at Battersea Polytechnic. His time at college resulted in a diploma qualification, although a degree was the desired outcome. Issigonis started working at Morris in 1936, and bolstered his experience by going racing and building a single-seater racing car, known as the Lightweight Special, by hand. With a job that was considered vitally important, he was excluded from being drafted to World War II, and in that time he worked on several military-related automobile projects.

Issigonis designed the Morris Minor, which would be a big seller throughout its lifespan. He designed it mostly by eye, and the central bonnet line was a result of him cutting the car in half and making it wider. However, despite this success, Issigonis is certainly more famous for creating the Mini, nearly a decade later.

Issigonis spent the vast majority of his life living with his mother, and never married. He was generally sociable and had time for other people's children – especially if they were interested in anything transport related. In his private life he was described as being highly intelligent, witty and charming, although he was rather more stubborn and arrogant in his professional life. He had no interest in market research or a committee of opinions, and is said to have based the Mini purely on his own experience as a driver and passenger.

When Morris merged with Austin in 1952, forming the British Motor Corporation (BMC), Issigonis looked for pastures new. He moved to Alvis, another British car company, and designed a luxurious saloon with a 3.5-litre V8 engine and the world's first hydraulic suspension system. He was brought back to BMC three years later, however, primarily to design a family-size car as well as a small car to sit below the Minor. His solitary approach to car design wasn't welcomed by some people he worked for, so later in his career the projects he worked on became smaller and more restricted in scope.

Issigonis was awarded a knighthood in 1969, and retired two years later. However, he continued to act as a consultant to BMC (by then called British Leyland), until his death in 1988.

BELOW: Issigonis was tasked with creating the Mini after the 1956 Suez crisis, when there was a shortage of oil and fuel became very expensive.

BELOW: The Mini
measured just over
three metres in
length, yet managed
to fit in an engine,
space for four and a
good-sized boot.

Issigonis and his friend Dr Alex Moulton looked to the
Citroën 2CV for inspiration when it came to the suspension
for the Mini. They wanted to recreate its smooth ride and grip,
but also to build a car with far less body roll than the wallowy
Citroën. This Hydrolastic system was not in fact ready in time
for the Mini's launch in 1959, but was made available five years
later. Instead, Moulton designed a clever yet simple suspension
setup, consisting of rubber cones to replace the conventional
springs. The suspension was "progressive", so it was pliant over
small bumps and a bit firmer at higher speeds, and allowed
the Mini to cope with a wide range of weights; fully laden,
it was around 400kg (882lb), or 70 per cent, heavier than
when unladen.

The wheels were pushed right out to the corners to
maximize interior space, and allowed the added appeal of quick
and agile handling. It is commonly said but true: the Mini felt
like a go kart. Tiny 25-cm (10-inch) wheels were specified to
keep as much space as possible, which meant new tyres had

ABOVE: The Mini was designed with a fold-down tailgate, so you could carry bulkier items than the boot could accommodate.

to be created by Dunlop. After the wheel size was agreed, it's reported that Issigonis tried to get even smaller 20-cm (eight-inch) wheels fitted to the Mini. By way of comparison, most modern family cars sit on wheels at least twice that size.

It looks as though the Mini should be a hatchback, with its flat rear end, but it's classified as a saloon because the boot opening doesn't include the rear windscreen. Issigonis designed the car as a saloon all along, but didn't want the Mini to look like a traditional "three-box" saloon with a boot sticking out of the back. Luggage space wasn't really a concern, as too much cargo capacity would make the car bigger than it needed to be, but the 195-litre (6.8-cu ft) boot was still a good size; it's more than a modern Toyota Aygo offers. You could flip the

RIGHT: The Mini's body shell was incredibly light, weighing just 140kg (309lb). The whole car weighed around 600kg (1,322lb) – around half the weight of a small modern car.

boot lid down and use it as a tray for bulky items, while most Minis came with big door bins, a full-width dashboard shelf and stowage space under the rear seats. It is said that the door bins were the perfect size to fit the ingredients for Issigonis' favourite dry Martini cocktail.

It's also rumoured that Issigonis deliberately designed the seats to be uncomfortable, to keep drivers alert, and that he never designed the car to feature a radio because it wasn't something he enjoyed listening to – which goes some

way to suggesting how much this was Issigonis' project, and his alone.

A Mini is instantly recognizable (and the design itself was later trademarked), but its external seams and door handles were actually included just for simplicity. Issigonis never saw himself as a car designer or an architect – instead, in an interview in his later years, he referred to himself as an ironmonger. The car's styling was purely a result of its packaging, he said, although the front end does bear some resemblance to his previous design, the

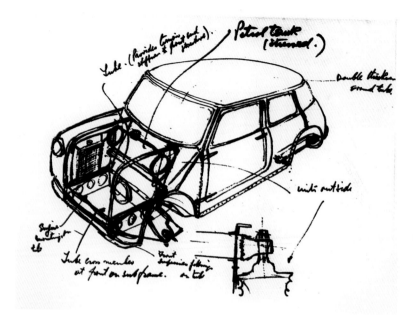

Luke. (Provide taping but upper & find junker). Petrol tank (screened.)

Double thicken round tube.

mini outside

Engine on stringer tb

Tube cross member at front on subframe.

Front suspension fittings. on tb

ABOVE: The original Mini prototype used a 38hp engine, which was good for a 93mph top speed. That was considered too fast, so a smaller engine was used.

OPPOSITE: The Longbridge factory built Minis right up until 2000, but it was also built at Oxford and at many sites internationally.

Morris Minor. Issigonis said that fashion dates, but logic doesn't; given that the Mini looks just as good today as it always has done, that point may ring true.

Leonard Lord also hated bubble cars for their lacklustre performance, and wanted much better performance for the Mini. But the 38hp 0.9-litre engine in original prototypes was deemed too powerful for the Mini's needs, as it could hit over 145kmh (90mph). Tweaks to the engine reduced it in size, power dropped to 34hp and there was much less torque. With these changes, the Mini still managed up to 120kmh (75mph), which was more than you could expect from most small cars of the era. Up until then, there had been no real need for cars to go so fast, as the UK's first stretch of motorway only opened in December 1958. However, faster Minis weren't very far away.

MAJOR SUCCESS FOR THE MINIATURE CAR

TURBULENT TIMES AND NEW RIVALS

BMC boss Leonard Lord wanted the Mini in production in just two years, which would be quite a challenge even now. But Issigonis and his small team managed it, and the car was launched on 26 August 1959. Because BMC comprised two car brands, a version of the Mini was sold under each one. If you were keen on Morrises, you'd want the Morris Mini-Minor, while Austin aficionados would go for the Austin Seven (an indirect replacement for the affordable and tiny Austin 7). Apart from minor cosmetic tweaks, the two vehicles were identical.

Each came in two trim levels – but the Mini was always conceived to be inexpensive. It featured cables instead of door handles and sliding windows as opposed to wind-down versions, in order to save both on cost and weight. The Mini was marketed as affordable motoring and was one of the cheapest cars on sale. It was priced similarly to the Ford Popular, which was an incredibly basic car that had its roots in the early 1930s. Popular it was, modern it certainly wasn't…

OPPOSITE: Directors and factory staff celebrate the production of the two millionth Mini in June 1969.

ABOVE: The classic Mini was priced to compete against the Ford Popular (or Pop, as it was often called), even though the Mini was a much more sophisticated car.

Nevertheless, the Mini wasn't cheap to develop, as all the innovative and space-saving ideas ended up coming at a cost. In fact, the Mini always struggled to make money throughout its 41-year-long production run. Many of its rivals were more expensive, so it's likely that the Mini would have racked up nearly as many sales – perhaps even more – had it been priced to compete with its main competitors, rather than the cheapest models.

Ford even took a Mini and reverse-engineered it, and figured that BMC must have been making losses of six per cent on every Mini produced. It took Ford until the 1970s to produce a real Mini rival, the Fiesta; before that it relied on the much larger Cortina to account for the majority of its sales. The Cortina name sounded exotic (it was apparently named after the Italian ski resort Cortina d'Ampezzo) but in Spanish it meant something rather more mundane: curtain.

BMC said profits came from the high-spec Cooper and Cooper S models, plus optional extras. And you would want to spend a bit more than the original £497 starting price when the base Mini was sold without a heater, radio, seat belts or door mirrors!

Sales of the Mini were initially slow and, on top of that, BMC had to iron out a few rather pressing issues early in the car's life. One was that the floor would get flooded with water when it rained, as some body parts were poorly designed and essentially scooped water up into the cabin. This made it smell as if someone had let a pack of wet dogs go wild inside. The issues often came about because of the Mini's short development time, but 80 early Minis were given to motoring journalists to test for a year, so any faults could be rectified. Many then bought the car after their loans had come to an end. One journalist was even tasked with driving 8,200 miles around the Mediterranean, which enabled faults to be found and fixed.

BELOW: It would take Ford until the mid-1970s to create a real rival for the Mini – the first Fiesta. Until then it had relied on sales of the bigger Cortina.

RIGHT: The Cooper
S was replaced by
the 1275 GT in 1969,
packing a much
bigger engine –
although still with
just 59hp.

One person to get a sneak peek of the Mini before
it was revealed was John Cooper, a racing driver whose
name would go on to be used on sportier versions of the
car throughout much of its lifespan. He was a friend of
Alec Issigonis and immediately saw the Mini's potential
as a sports car, with its light weight, short wheelbase and

agile handling. The upgraded 55hp Mini Cooper came out two years after the car's launch, and was soon joined by an even faster Cooper S, which had a bigger engine with 70hp and a 159kmh (99mph) top speed. It might not sound like much, but the Mini would go on to become an incredibly successful racing car.

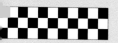

Sporty Minis have long carried the Cooper name, and the hottest new MINI models continue to sit under the John Cooper Works banner. Born in Surrey in 1923, John Cooper would go on to set up the Cooper Car Company with his father, Charles. The family firm built racing cars, models which used a rear-engined chassis design that would eventually change both Formula 1 and Indy 500 cars.

John Cooper used to race the cars himself but, as the company grew, he became too busy to compete. In the early 1950s there was a long line of aspiring young racers keen on Cooper cars, including Sir Stirling Moss and Bruce McLaren. The brand racked up 16 Formula 1 Grand Prix wins and two back-to-back World Championships by the end of the decade.

Cooper became a friend of Alec Issigonis when the two were racing against each other, and also bought BMC engines for his race cars. While Issigonis was fixated on the Mini being an affordable car for the people, Cooper could see that it would make an excellent sports car. The Mini Cooper S would chalk up three Monte Carlo rally wins throughout the 1960s, and consistently humbled more powerful and expensive machinery.

Before his death in late 2000, Cooper's name was licensed to BMW so faster MINIs could still wear the famous badge, and he worked as an advisor on the design of the BMW-built car. He was rather more positive about it than Dr Alex Moulton, that's for sure.

OPPOSITE: John Cooper started tuning Minis even before they were launched – he saw the Mini as an ideal sports car.

In the mid-1960s, the Mini was endowed with two new options to further broaden its appeal. One was BMC's Hydrolastic suspension system that was designed to give a softer ride, using fluids instead of the standard rubber cone setup – although this was only available until 1971. You could also order a four-speed "Mini-matic" automatic gearbox from 1965, a feature that had previously been reserved for high-end luxury cars.

A few big changes were introduced in 1969, when conventional winding windows were fitted in place of space-saving sliding types, and the door hinges started to be mounted on the inside of the car. Meanwhile, a fall-out in BMC would see the Cooper name axed for a 21-year period.

The popularity of the Mini continued to grow in the early 1970s, hitting two million sales in 1969, and three and four million sales by 1972 and 1976. Production peaked in 1971

BELOW: Four years after the Mini's 50th birthday, the Porsche 911 celebrated the same anniversary. Both are icons of the 20th century, despite having very different purposes and power outputs.

at 320,000 cars, amid a turbulent economy; the '70s would come to be known for strikes, inflation and a shortage of oil. British Leyland (the successor to BMC) was bailed out by the government, and simultaneously gained an unwanted reputation for poor-quality cars. Its tiniest offering would face competition from newcomers like the Renault 5, Vauxhall Chevette and Ford Fiesta, which were all fitted with a more useful hatchback boot.

By the 1980s, the Mini looked to be on its last legs. Only 70,000 Minis were built in 1981, a stark contrast to a decade before, as the Austin Mini-Metro was launched at the start of the '80s. The Metro had been intended to replace the Mini, but actually ended up sitting alongside it – although it did essentially replace the larger Austin Allegro.

1984 marked the Mini's 25th anniversary, and a special-edition Mini 25 model was launched. It was a better idea than

cake and party hats, as it essentially brought the Mini into a new light. There had been the odd special edition before this one, but it kicked off a huge number of limited-production models that would be used as a selling tactic right up until the car was finally discontinued in 2000. Rather than being seen as outdated, the Mini acquired a nostalgic, retro image, and buyers found it more appealing as a result.

The Mini 25 came in metallic silver paint with grey and red stripes and number '25' logos. There was also luxury velvet upholstery with red seatbelts, red piping and a leather steering wheel, plus a cassette player, wheel arch extensions, a door mirror on each side and a certificate of authenticity. Special editions followed to mark the car's 30th, 35th and 40th anniversaries, each limited to just a couple of thousand cars worldwide.

The evocative names of upmarket London districts and landmarks were often used as inspiration for limited-run Minis, such as Chelsea, Park Lane and Ritz. The late 1980s also saw a wide range of colour-specific special editions, but each and every one came with a unique trim and colour combination. Fashion designers Paul Smith and Mary Quant also had their own limited editions, while many more were spun off the faster Cooper model. In 1991 continental Europe even got a special version with *After Eight* chocolate branding.

In retrospect, it's no wonder the Mini cost so much to build when the production line had to accommodate so many small-volume versions.

The endless stream of special editions no doubt helped the Mini reach over 5.3 million sales globally, but BMC's and British Leyland's advertising departments never really made an effort to get cars out of the showroom. Perhaps they didn't need to. British adverts for the Mini focused on practical reasons to buy the car, such as its fuel economy and the fact that it was

OPPOSITE: The Mini and the Palace of Westminster – a pair of British icons.

OVERLEAF: The Knightsbridge was one of several late-era Minis to take its name from a fashionable district of London.

ABOVE: The Mini
Cooper name
returned in the
1990s, and by
1992 all cars were
fuel injected as
the Mini tried to
meet increasingly
stringent emissions
regulations.

so easy to park, only occasionally using celebrities like Twiggy and James Bolam. Often, the advert simply showed a car in a blank studio, too, with a meaty chunk of text beneath. While the British attempts were sometimes half-baked and even confusing, the Australian versions were a bit more colourful. The Mini would be pictured with boats and young surfer-type models under a perfect blue sky, playing on the fun aspect of the car.

Safety was never really mentioned in these adverts, because the Mini's safety record had never been great. "I don't design my car to have accidents", Issigonis claimed, adding that the car had "such good brakes, such good steering, that if people get into a crash it's their own fault". One point of view, certainly – but it is hard to avoid someone else crashing into you. Safety experts were concerned about the protruding door handles and fuel filler cap, so BMC changed these in the mid-1960s, while the engine did sometimes intrude dangerously into the passenger space in a collision. Throughout its lifespan, the Mini flirted with new safety regulations several times, and each time it seemed that the car might have to be taken off the market. Airbags were finally introduced in 1996, alongside side-impact bars, and BMW managed to make the Mini comply for another four years until it was pensioned off.

America banned the Mini over safety concerns as early as 1968, while Canadians could buy the car up until 1980. However, questions over the car's crash performance didn't stop it becoming one of the bestselling cars of all time, nor the fact that hundreds of kit cars and variants were based upon it.

BELOW: Mini advertisements ranged widely from sparse, minimal posters to more elaborate, illustrated affairs such as this example.

AUSTIN Incredible **m i n i** Saloon....

★ Combined ignition/starter switch.
★ Safety sun visors and interior mirror.
★ Two-leading-shoe brakes at front.
★ Greater torque capacity gearbox.

...now with Hydrolastic suspension!

A MINI FOR
EVERYONE

BRANCHING OUT

Successful products and businesses adapt to changing times, in order to remain relevant and cater for new customer demands. On the face of it, the Mini didn't really change much over its mammoth production run – at least not in terms of styling. The round headlights, squat bonnet and square windows were there from the start – and still there right at the end, when the last Mini rolled off the production line on 4 October 2000.

But this humble box on wheels, designed to give proper motoring to the masses, would spawn an absurdly wide variety of cars. You could have an estate, a pickup truck, a sporty version and, if you lived in selected countries, a Mini created in a different material entirely. And that's just those models created and licensed by BMC; *hundreds* of other kit cars and shed projects have used the underpinnings of a Mini.

The Mini's development process was incredibly short – it was on sale just two years after work started on it – and it would be a similarly rapid process to bring several Mini-based variants to market.

OPPOSITE: One of the secrets to the Mini's success was its potential for personalization, despite a lack of diversity in its underlying styling.

OPPOSITE: The
Riley Elf was spun
off the Mini; it was
very similar but it
was thought it would
capture sales from
fans of the Riley
brand. Wolseley
made its own version,
called the Hornet.

OVERLEAF: Like the
Mini hatchback, the
estate came in two
versions – the Morris
Mini Traveller and
the Austin Seven
Countryman.

RILEY ELF AND WOLSELEY HORNET

Among the first of these were the Riley Elf and Wolseley Hornet. Both companies were owned by Morris, so fell under the BMC umbrella. They also both marketed a plusher version of the Mini, with a larger grille, fancier bumpers and a bigger boot at the back if you wanted something a bit smarter than the basic model. The Riley was the more expensive of the two, and it featured a proper dashboard rather than just an empty shelf. Initially, both used the same 34hp engine as the Mini, but two years into production they received the more powerful engine from the original Mini prototypes, with the brakes thankfully being improved as well. Wind-up windows and the door hinges were introduced two years before they were added to the base Mini, but both models were phased out before the start of the 1970s.

MINI ESTATE

Slightly predating the Elf and Hornet were estate versions of the Mini, launched in 1960 as the Morris Mini Traveller and the Austin Mini Countryman. You might think an estate, or wagon, built on one the tiniest cars available may have been a silly idea, but some 200,000 were sold before these also were withdrawn from the market in 1969. The estate versions of the Mini had a longer chassis and most came with decorative wood trim on the rear sections – although standard versions were also available without this feature.

Wizardry at work again!

QUALITY FI

THE MORI

PUBLICATION No. H. & E. 62107

 MINI-TRAVELLER

ABOVE: The Mini Van and estate versions were based on the same car, but the van came with blanked-out rear windows and no rear seats.

MINI VAN AND PICKUP

There was also a Mini van, and even a Mini pickup truck, which were launched in the early 1960s but continued on until 1983. Both used the longer chassis from the estates, and came with simple metal holes at the front of the engine bay instead of a proper grille, in order to save costs. Half a million vans were sold because, in the carefree days before seatbelts and pesky child safety regulations, the van was a popular alternative to a normal car; it was cheaper and wasn't taxed as heavily.

BELOW: Originally
designed for military
use, the Mini Moke
buggy became
popular in sunny
countries such as the
United States and
Australia.

MINI MOKE

If you didn't care too much for weather protection, the Mini
Moke might have been up your street. With four-wheel drive,
two engines and the ability to scale a 1:2 gradient, it was
originally conceived for military use, but the poor ground
clearance meant it was never used in battle. Instead, a two-
wheel drive version with just the one engine became a cult hit
in sunny coastal areas of America and Australia. Speaking
of Aussies, a "Mini K" was available down under from
1969–71, built using 80 per cent local materials; the "K" stood
for "kangaroo".

OPPOSITE: Buyers
wanted a yet-faster
version of the Mini,
so the Cooper S
was launched with
70hp. It could hit
a top speed of
99mph, which was
incredibly fast in the
early 1960s.

MINI COOPER AND COOPER S

The best-known of all Minis were the Cooper and Cooper S models, however. These featured more power than the standard 34hp car, with the Cooper S packing double the oomph of entry-level models. The Cooper was originally limited to 1,000 cars, while the BMC management worked out if it was a good idea or not. Some 80,000 were eventually sold, with a further 25,000 Cooper S cars built in the initial ten-year production run.

The Cooper models were replaced, somewhat controversially, by the Mini 1275 GT in 1971. Sir Donald Stokes (who would later become a Lord) was running British Leyland at this time. He was primarily a salesman and seemed to have little knowledge of how to run a car company, especially one as big and fragmented as BL. Misguidedly, Stokes decided that BL didn't need to employ John Cooper as a consultant, because the company already employed around 150,000 people. The result was that the Cooper name was shelved for over 20 years and, while it saved a little bit of money in royalties, Mini also lost the famous branding that had been so successful for many years.

The 1275 GT was given slightly more power than the Cooper (59hp vs 55hp) but couldn't match the Cooper S for pace. It would still top out at 145kmh (90mph), though, and its 12-second 100kmh (0-62mph) time is better than many modern city cars today – and no doubt it would have felt a lot quicker, as the driver was so low to the ground in a Mini. Insurance and running costs were cheaper than the Cooper S, if that was any consolation.

Like the Mini Clubman it was based upon, the sporty new model featured a sharp front end that brought better crash protection (but worse aerodynamics), while the 1275 GT was the first Mini to feature a rev counter. It was also the first

ABOVE: A Mini Convertible was built in Germany in 1991, and the Rover Group liked it so much that it bought the tooling Around 1,000 were sold between 1993-96.

production car to wear run-flat tyres, which are designed to allow you to continue driving when you have a puncture. The square face of the car was meant to replace the more rounded look of earlier Minis, but the two were produced side-by-side throughout the 1970s – and the rounded look ended up being used all the way through the Mini's life.

The Mini Cooper name was revived in 1990, and by 1992 all cars got a fuel-injected 1.3-litre engine (which, besides the fuel injection, was the same as it had been all those years before). The Cooper name would become an essential part of the branding of the new MINI, which was launched around a decade later.

MINIS BUILT OVERSEAS

While the bulk of all Minis were built in either Cowley (Oxford) or Longbridge (Birmingham), some were constructed in more exotic regions. Innocenti, the makers of Lambretta scooters, built the Mini under licence in Italy until 1975 – and they probably would have continued had British Leyland (formerly BMC) not been nationalized. Innocenti Minis were built from kits exported from England, although the shells and some components had to be produced locally. When the partnership with BL ended, Innocenti produced a new "Mini" with the help of supercar builder De Tomaso. An unlikely partnership, you might think… The result was an incredibly boxy small car that was clearly a product of the 1970s, which would actually be sold right up until the brand was discontinued by Fiat in the 1990s.

Minis were also built in Pamplona, Spain, by Authi. A collaboration between BMC and a local metal working company, the Authi project was created so that BMC could sell cars in the Iberian peninsula. The Authi Minis often received more equipment than British-built versions, including a walnut dashboard and leather seats. Production only lasted for seven years, however, before British Leyland collapsed, taking Authi with it.

In total, the Mini was sold in around 100 countries, but it never caught on particularly well in South America. Cars were built in Chile for five years from 1969, but were made of fibreglass – a material more commonly used to build canoes. Fibreglass is a very resilient material that doesn't break down easily, so the body shells will last far longer than the rest of the car. Venezuelan company Facorca then had another go at fibreglass Minis in 1990, but the production run was even shorter, spanning just four years. In that time, it's thought that only around 1,300 were produced, with many staying in the country and some being exported to neighbouring Colombia.

CARS BASED ON MINIS

Like a song that gets jumped on and remixed endlessly by producers, the Mini became the foundation for an absolutely vast number of other models. The Mini's dazzling handling and peppy engine appealed, as did the fact that it was readily available. Most cars spun off from a Mini were kit cars or low-volume sports cars, built in much smaller facilities than actual BMC cars – very often just sheds.

Marcos, a company known for its racing and sports cars – at least, when it was actually in business – built the Mini Marcos, which also used a lightweight fibreglass body on top of the Mini's running gear. It had a much longer bonnet than the car it was based on, and a heavily chopped roof, so was sleeker and more aerodynamic than the original car.

The Unipower GT is reasonably well-known, too, even though only around 70 were built in the late 1960s. This was a car that was designed by the same man who conceived the Ford GT40, and the shape was even approved by Issigonis himself. It was usually sold as a completed car, but if you looked under the bonnet you wouldn't find an engine – the Unipower GT was mid-engined, with the Cooper or Cooper S engine thrumming away just behind the seats.

Many spin-off models tried to mask their origins, but the Broadspeed GT embraced the donor car. Broadspeed was a racing team that had previously had success with Minis, and had produced tuning parts for them, so its closeness to the proper Mini was maybe not so surprising. A swoopy new fibreglass panel was fitted in place of the rear section, giving it a much sportier look. Some said it looked like a scaled-down Aston Martin.

Not all models were sports cars, though. In fact, dream up anything that might be based on a Mini and it will probably already exist. There were early, rudimentary electric

OPPOSITE: One of the most athletic-looking Mini-based cars was the Mini Marcos, which used a fibreglass body. It was the only British car to finish in the 1966 Le Mans 24-hour race.

conversions, Mini Moke knock-offs and even campervan conversions. Yes, some people decided that one of the smallest cars on sale would be the perfect base for a camper. Windswept escapes to the coast must have been pretty cosy!

At this point we should also mention William Towns, a British car designer responsible for the svelte Aston Martin DBS and the rather more boxy Aston Martin Lagonda. When setting up his own design studio after leaving Aston Martin, he really embraced the boxy theme, designing several bizarre-looking cars (just boxes, really), all based on the Mini, named the Hustler, the Minissima and the Microdot. The Hustler even came with a choice of four or six wheels, plus MPV, convertible and wheelchair-accessible versions. Apparently – perhaps incredibly – around 500 people were sufficiently interested to actually buy one of these golf-cart lookalikes.

LEFT: The Broadspeed GT was a Birmingham-built car with a much sportier-looking rear end than the standard Mini.

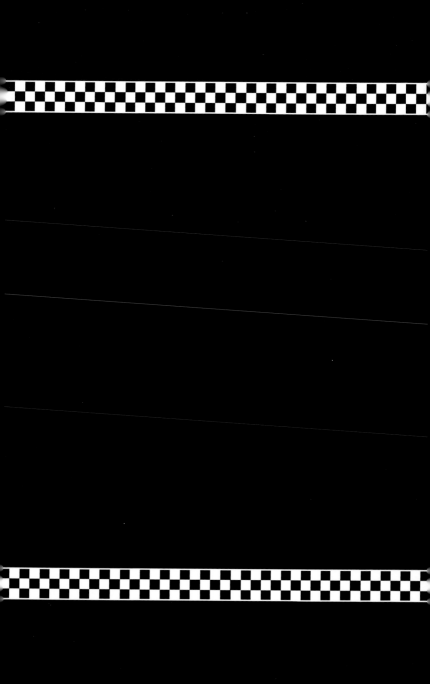

TRENDSETTER,
FILM STAR, ICON

FINDING FAME AT HOME AND ABROAD

According to a famous saying, new is always better – but new is scary, too. Something different or revolutionary may not always catch on, and the public can be sceptical or confused in their first responses. The distinctly different Renault Avantime and Audi A2 are both proof of that. The Mini never sold particularly well at the outset, partly because it was a completely new idea.

The Mini was also launched as one of the cheapest cars on the road, because Alec Issigonis had designed it first and foremost as mass transportation – giving working-class people the chance to move away from motorbikes or bubble cars. Even the Isetta and Messerschmitt "cars" were more expensive, and you only got two seats in those. But, being so clearly targeted, most lower-income Britons initially just said, "No, thanks" to the Mini, or perhaps something ruder. People wanted aspirational cars, just as they do now, and the Mini was overlooked at first precisely because it was so inexpensive to buy.

OPPOSITE: Noted Mini owner John Lennon drives a psychedelic Radford Mini de Ville during filming for The Beatles' TV film *Magical Mystery Tour*.

However, things soon changed when film stars, socialites and even royalty took to the Mini. Sure, these people could all afford much more expensive cars – but the Mini was the perfect vehicle to thread through sticky London traffic. The Mini fitted in and looked the part everywhere, whether it was parked outside Buckingham palace, a designer boutique or a fish and chip shop. It became classless.

On quiet evenings, London's Belgrave Square became the unofficial street circuit for the Mini's wealthy owners. You can imagine the drivers' smiles as manic tyre screeches were heard long into the night – and the only way the police could bring the mischief to a halt was by getting their own Mini Cooper to give chase.

So let's take a look at some of those Mini-owning trendsetters, to whom the little car really owes its success. The Mini became a must-have accessory for the likes of Twiggy, Jenny Agutter and Lulu, as well as Princess Margaret – the Queen's sister, no less – who was royally charmed by the characterful little box on wheels. Further afield, other regal owners included the Royal Family of Brunei (usually known for their exotic supercar collections) and Princess Grace of Monaco, who would often take her Mini around the Monte Carlo hills. Maybe she was practising to try and beat Paddy Hopkirk and Rauno Aaltonen – but more on those two later.

Actor Peter Sellers must have been one of the biggest fans of this smallest of cars. The *Goon Show* and *Pink Panther* star saw fit to have bespoke wicker panelling and a custom interior by coachwork company Hooper added to his Mini, which made the car four times more expensive than a normal, bog-standard version. There were extremely plush leather reclining seats, a mahogany dashboard and a bang-up-to-date radio. Coachbuilding company Radford recreated the car for the *Pink Panther* sequel, and it was exported to California before

OPPOSITE: The London-to-Brighton Mini run has become a celebrated part of the line-up, and in 2009 a new world record was set - with a convoy of 1,450 Minis!

ABOVE: The Mini was favoured by celebrities and VIPs as well as ordinary people – and all the Beatles had Minis. A couple of them were made to be unique.

being brought back to its home country for a full restoration in the 1990s. In total, it's thought Sellers owned a dozen or so Minis throughout his lifetime.

MUSICAL MINIS

As legend has it, the most expensive Mini ever built was commissioned by Monkees guitar wrangler Mike Nesmith. It was sent to Radford and famous Mini tuners Downton, and ended up having exclusive seats and instruments, plus a tape deck and a unique ventilation system, as well as a 100hp engine. Metallic paint and pink upholstery were fitted, and the end result cost around £3,640 in 1967 (over £67,500 in today's money).

An even bigger band in the 1960s made the Mini a true style icon. Each member of The Beatles was given a Mini by their band manager, Brian Epstein, in 1965, and each one was as different as the next. Paul McCartney's featured Aston Martin rear lights and the company's sage-green metallic paint, plus fog lights, halogen headlights and an interior completely upholstered in black leather. A crash on an icy road saw it written off and, since then, conspiracy theorists have been convinced that McCartney died in the accident and was replaced by an impostor.

George Harrison's Mini was painted red and gold with a suitably psychedelic decoration. It featured a full-length sunroof and fog lights which, for some reason, were mounted on the bonnet. Eric Clapton owned it for a while, too. John Lennon's Mini was completely blacked out; it's thought his ended up in the hands of his butler in America. Lennon was known for being a bad driver, and only held his licence for four years.

Before his time narrating *Thomas the Tank Engine* cartoons, Ringo Starr owned a Mini like no other. It was converted to a

BELOW: The new MINIs were often used as promotional vehicles, such as the Red Bull MINIs. These had the rear end cut out and a large Red Bull energy drink can mounted to the roof.

HOB 446L

hatchback in order to accommodate his drum kit, and had a two-tone paint scheme using selections from Rolls-Royce's colour palette. At an auction in 2017 it was passed on to a member of another massive British band – Geri Halliwell of the Spice Girls, who is said to have paid £102,000 for this small slice of Beatles history.

Celebrity-owned Minis often cost several times as much as a base-spec model, but that didn't mean Mini-modifying was an exclusive club. Long before the days of eBay car parts, you could customize your Mini in pretty much any way imaginable. Extra performance was easy to come by, if you took your car to Speedwell, Oselli, Taurus, Yimkin or hundreds of other tuners. You didn't have to call upon Downton like the stars did – the Sixties equivalent of around £500 bought tuning kits that would knock between five and eight seconds off the acceleration time and increase the top speed.

There were extended pedals for better heel-and-toeing (for pretending you're a racing driver), remote gearshift linkages, whitewall tyres, and a lot more besides. To make your Mini stand out even more, you could add light bars, leather bonnet straps, proper dashboards and even a cupholder. Shame the drive-through restaurant wouldn't make it over to Britain until 1986. To combat the lack of space, you could buy bulky extra luggage compartments and a roof-mounted tent, which probably seemed a silly idea back then but is an idea that is becoming popular again now.

LEFT: One of the more unusual cars to be based on the Mini was the Mini Outspan Orange, which was used for promotion. Only six were built, and one resides in the UK's Beaulieu Motor Museum.

FILM STAR

It wasn't just actors and musicians that made the Mini popular. Often, the car itself was the star, turning up in all sorts of films and TV shows.

You might remember Michael Caine saying, "You were only supposed to blow the bloody doors off!" in 1969's heist comedy *The Italian Job*, but let's face it – the trio of Mini Coopers was the most memorable aspect of the film. There were whispers of product placement, so that could have been entirely deliberate. It almost certainly was in the 2003 remake.

Minis were used in *The Italian Job* as they could slip through narrow alleys and tunnels, going into all the places where the chasing police could not. The little cars looked fantastic bouncing down staircases and doing handbrake turns in shopping centres with particularly greasy floors, especially with the rally-style ancillary lights and leather bonnet straps. Maybe they had raided the options list for strengthening beams too, as the Minis would have had to cope with more than their weight in gold.

You would have expected a special-edition Mini to celebrate its big-screen moment, right? There was one, but only 23 years after the film had first been released. Obviously you could have the Italian Job edition painted in red, white or blue like the film cars (or British Racing Green), and all had the spotlights and bonnet stripes, plus small decals and flags dotted around. There were 1,000 units made for British buyers, and 750 for the Italian market.

Fast-forward to January 1991 and the Mini would be the star of an altogether different show. Rowan Atkinson's hapless Mr Bean character became well-known for driving a bright green Mini with a matte black bonnet – even if the very first one was orange. The Minis used in the show tended to have a padlock on the driver's side, and Mr Bean would remove

OPPOSITE: The Mini had plenty of on-screen time, and attracted young fans with its starring role in *Mr Bean*.

ABOVE: Spies usually have cars that can blend in with traffic so they can go about their duties without being spotted. Not so in *Austin Powers*, where a Union Jack-emblazoned MINI Cooper was used.

the steering wheel as an anti-theft precaution. Whether he was getting dressed in the Mini, putting a television on the roof, transporting an oversized Christmas tree or steering the car from an armchair, Mr Bean entertained kids and adults around the globe, and always had a teddy bear by his side for company.

Those were arguably the car's most famous on-screen appearances, but they weren't the only ones. Far, far from it. The Mini played the main role in *Goodbye Pork Pie*, a film with all the normal road movie clichés – handbrake turns, the police being strangely unable to stop a car's progress, and a bit where a car ends up in a train carriage – except it was produced in New Zealand. The Mini seemed to outgun and outwit a host of V8-engined cop cars, while driving through some of the country's pretty scenery. No wonder *Goodbye Pork Pie* is sometimes considered New Zealand's most iconic film.

The Mini also showed up in *The Bourne Identity, Austin Powers, The Prisoner, Stormbreaker* and countless other films. It would also feature in plenty of TV shows, such as *Top Gear*, in which a Mini was used as a rocket-powered ski jump vehicle in 2004. Another one, this time a gorgeous late-model Mini Cooper, was one of the main cars in the show's India special eight years later. After the normal *Top Gear* chaos, it would end up getting its face torn off when trying to winch a Rolls-Royce Silver Shadow up a steep mountain pass.

The car's iconic status had been clear for a long time, and in 1995 the Mini won *Autocar* magazine's Car of the Century award. Four years later, its 40th birthday celebrations included input from the likes of supermodel Kate Moss and legendary rock star David Bowie. Moss's had a cobweb effect; Bowie's used polished chrome bodywork and reflective glass. He compared it to a sandwich for its classic design and its fitness for purpose. Bowie not only owned a Mini, but worked on the BMC production line in the 1960s.

BELOW: Pop star David Bowie created a one-off chrome Mini in 1998.

A MINI MOTORSPORT LEGEND

GIANT KILLER

You could be forgiven for writing the Mini off, as so many people did at the time. It wasn't powerful, sat on tiny wheels and not much thought had been given to its aerodynamics. Front-wheel drive made it unique amongst rear-drive competitors, however, and the Mini would soon show its skills – and show up much more powerful machines. It would win three Monte Carlo rallies throughout the 1960s, as well as countless other events.

While Alec Issigonis always said he had never considered that the Mini would become a successful racing car, John Cooper most certainly did. Early prototypes for road-going cars were said to be too powerful, but Cooper was already thinking of how to make the Mini faster and more suited to racing – even before the car was launched. With each wheel pushed right out to the corners and not a lot of weight, the Mini was agile yet stable – and it could clearly handle more power.

OPPOSITE: John Cooper used to race his own cars, and the Cooper racing cars were also driven by famous names such as Jack Brabham and Sir Stirling Moss.

The Mini was launched in late August in 1959, and even before the end of the year a Mini had finished first in its class at a saloon car racing event at Snetterton circuit. It wasn't particularly fast in a straight line – you might have guessed that – but it was phenomenal in the corners. Like the production cars, early Mini racers weren't always reliable, and the extra forces from high-speed cornering tested some components to their limits. Exhaust pipes would often break, while the prolonged stress of endurance events caused front wheels to fly off. Of all the components on the car, the wheels are probably high on the list of ones you

would like to stay in place. But it wasn't an isolated issue; it happened so often that any Minis still on their original wheels were banned from UK motorsport events.

But it was rallying for which the Mini was really known, even with its limited ground clearance. Minis were also racing in rallies right from the very first year of production, and an outright win came as early as 1962. Pat Moss, with co-driver Ann Riley, led the field of the Tulip Rally in the Netherlands in a Mini Cooper. It was the precursor to a number of rally wins that decade.

BELOW: Pat Moss & Ann Wisdom-Riley collect their trophies with their Morris Mini Cooper during the 1962 Monte Carlo Rally.

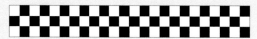

MAKERS OF THE MINI – PAT MOSS

With five European Ladies' Rally championships and three outright rally victories to her name, Pat Moss should certainly be more well known. She was one of the most successful female drivers of all time, which perhaps isn't a surprise given her father was a racing driver and her brother was Sir Stirling Moss. She died of cancer in 2008 at her home in Bedfordshire.

As a BMC works driver, Pat Moss raced MG TFs, Morris Minors and Austin-Healeys before the "twitchy" Mini Cooper. Moss joined Saab in 1964, a year after marrying famous Saab racing driver Erik Carlsson (who won the Monte Carlo rally in 1962 and 1963). Carlsson was one of the first four drivers inducted into the Rally Hall of Fame, alongside Paddy Hopkirk, Rauno Aaltonen and Timo Mäkinen.

LEFT: Perhaps not such a household name, but Pat Moss was one of the most successful female racing drivers of all time.

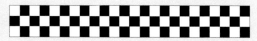

The Mini Cooper was a decent racing car, but the Cooper S was a brilliant one. After the switch was made in 1963, intentions turned to outright wins instead of just class victories. The team was starting to look more professional, too, and ushered in new practices that would become standard for most teams. Results did not take long to materialize.

Back then, the Monte Carlo rally didn't start in Monaco. In 1964 it commenced in nine cities across Europe, with racers having to drive essentially non-stop to then converge on the glitzy principality. So not only did Paddy Hopkirk win the event at Monte Carlo, but he raced from Minsk (now in Belarus, then Russia) in order to do so. A whopping 277 cars started the event, and Hopkirk's Mini was playing leapfrog with Bo Ljungfeldt's 300hp Ford Falcon throughout the stages, eventually pipping it for the victory. A combination of pre-written ice notes, the right tyres and the Mini's light weight and compact size made it unassailable on the snowy sections. The glamour of the Monte Carlo rally meant it made front-page headlines as well as being covered on the sports pages, so the Mini got plenty of well-deserved coverage.

"Win on Sunday, sell on Monday" is a saying that doesn't really apply so much now (it's unlikely that Colin Turkington winning a BTCC race weekend would spur people on to buy a BMW 1 Series), but it really did happen in the 1960s. After the rally, French dealers ordered more Minis than ever before, and a BMC report showed that UK Mini sales were up 53 per cent on the previous year.

OPPOSITE: 1967 was the last year that a Mini won the Monte Carlo rally, but it would continue to be successful in other forms of motorsport.

MAKERS OF THE MINI – PADDY HOPKIRK MBE

Belfast-born Paddy Hopkirk became an overnight success when he won the 1964 Monte Carlo rally. Not only was he booked up for a long string of interviews and media appearances, but he received a telegram from the Prime Minister of the time and a signed photo from The Beatles to celebrate his success. He'd joined BMC to drive the big Healey sports cars, and initially thought the Mini was "bloody awful" – until he drove it.

Hopkirk's early life wasn't so showbiz, and his first car wasn't really a car at all; aged 9, he was gifted an invalid carriage in a will, and learnt car control on that. Post-university, Hopkirk worked for Volkswagen in Ballsbridge, Dublin, where he had opportunities to buy old VW Beetles in which he went racing.

Like John Cooper, Hopkirk became an advisor to BMW when the new MINI was launched. In 2020 the brand launched a MINI Cooper S Paddy Hopkirk Edition, with the same colour scheme, grille-mounted fog lights and "37" decals – the same number as the winning car in 1964. Only 100 were made for the UK, but the car was available in 30 countries. Unfortunately, the coronavirus pandemic prevented Hopkirk from going on a world tour to promote it.

OPPOSITE: Paddy Hopkirk was the first to win a Monte Carlo rally in a Mini, and would have recorded a podium finish if the cars had not been disqualified in 1966.

BELOW: Timo Mäkinen and Paul Easter in their Mini Cooper S during the 1966 Monte Carlo rally. They were in first position overall, but were later disqualified for the use of illegal lights.

One Monte Carlo win was good. Two were better. In 1965 Timo Mäkinen clinched victory with a 1275cc Mini, but his bigger engine was offset by very tricky conditions. There was so much ice and snow that the cars might have been better off on skis, as well as an extra night stage through the Alps to make things even more difficult. How difficult? Out of the 237 cars that started the race, only 35 finished. Mäkinen was the only driver not to pick up penalty points, and won five of the six special stages towards the end of the rally.

1966 would have been the hat-trick, as well as a hat-trick on the podium, as Minis came in first, second and third place. Mäkinen, Aaltonen and Hopkirk beat every other car in the race – wowing the crowds at the event and at home on television – but all three were disqualified. Apparently this was due to their cars' lights not meeting regulations, although some suggested it was down to politics. Nothing changes. Other cars

were disqualified, too, and fifth-place Pauli Toivenen was awarded the (hollow) victory in a Citroën DS. Sure, the race win would have been remarkable, but it's likely that BMC got more publicity from being disqualified by the race organizers than if the original result had stood.

"The Three Musketeers", as they were imaginatively known, returned to the Monte Carlo rally in 1967 set on victory. Hopkirk had a win to his name, as did Mäkinen, so now it was Rauno Aaltonen's turn in the spotlight. He'd had to wait for his victory, not least because he was set to win the 1962 event until he rolled the Mini onto its roof just three kilometres (1.8 miles) from the finish line – and he had to be dragged out of the wrecked car. Alongside co-driver Henry Liddon – who had also been in the hot seat for Hopkirk's winning run – Aaltonen finished a healthy 12 seconds ahead of the next driver.

OVERLEAF: Minis seemed at home on any surface - be it tarmac, ice or gravel. The Mini enjoyed wins in many different racing disciplines.

MAKERS OF THE MINI – TIMO MÄKINEN

Finland produces far more than its fair share of rally drivers, due to the landscape of the country and because the Finnish driving test is vastly more rigorous than the British equivalent. Skid training is mandatory, and that comes in handy for people wanting to skid through forests at speed. In 1965 Mäkinen picked up a Rally Finland (known as the 1000 Lakes Rally then) win alongside his Monte Carlo triumph, and two years later he raced a Mini at the 1000 Lakes event with the bonnet open nearly the whole way. He had to keep the car sideways just to see where he was going! Mäkinen died in his native Helsinki in 2017.

BELOW: It was Timo Mäkinen's turn to win at the 1965 Monte Carlo rally, and he did finish first a year later - before the result was overturned.

MAKERS OF THE MINI – RAUNO AALTONEN

Another of the celebrated "Flying Finns" was Rauno Aaltonen, who had competed in speedboat racing before switching to cars. The son of a local garage owner, Aaltonen had a keen interest in machines, and started rallying in 1956. Before his Mini success, he had gained recognition on rally events in Poland and Finland. Throughout the 1960s, he had also competed in endurance racing, including at Le Mans and at Australia's infamously difficult Bathurst 1000 race. The 1965 Monte Carlo win was supplemented by eight other race wins and 14 class wins, making him the most successful driver of the Mini works team.

BELOW: Rauno Aaltonen drove Minis at Monte Carlo rallies throughout the 1960s, winning in 1967 and achieving two other podium finishes.

OPPOSITE: The late, great Niki Lauda started his racing career in a Mini at a hill climb event in his native Austria.

BELOW: As well as success in rallying, the Mini also won a number of touring car races, in the UK and overseas, in the 1960s.

The Mini's dominance in motor racing was coming to an end towards the later part of the 1960s, and by the start of the 1970s BMC had ceased entering works Minis in race events. But in 1968, a certain Niki Lauda started his racing career at the wheel of a Mini, at a hillclimb in the Austrian town of Linz. A second-place finish in that first race was succeeded by a win a fortnight later. Racing Minis was the catalyst to his career, which eventually included three Formula 1 World Championships.

Lauda wasn't the only future F1 supremo to start out in a Mini. It's a club that is also populated by Sir Jackie Stewart, John Surtees, Graham Hill, James Hunt and Jochen Rindt.

A racetrack was a semi-natural home for the Mini, too – not just dirt rallies. A Mini won the 1961 and 1962 British Saloon Car Championship (now the British Touring Car Championship), and further success would come in Belgium, Sweden, Germany and America in 1962. Race winners

included John Love, Sir John Whitmore, John Aley and Christabel Carlisle (who showed you didn't have to be called John to win). The same year of the first Monte Carlo rally win, Warwick Banks also won the European Saloon Car Championship in a 55hp Mini Cooper. Later success would come from John "Smokey" Rhodes, John Fitzpatrick and John Handley.

Despite seemingly being well past its best by the late '70s, Richard Longman won the BSCC in 1978 and '79 in a Downton-tuned Cooper S, but by then the Mini had seen its time up in motorsport. Nowadays, the Mini is a key part of historic races at events like the *Goodwood Revival.*

MOTORSPORT IN THE NEW MINI

BMW wasn't going to overlook the crucial role that motorsport had played in the original Mini's popularity, and having the John Cooper Works name at its disposal for the new MINI meant it could go wild. The JCW versions of the MINI are the hottest, and the fastest on a racetrack, and even these have motorsport pedigree to back them up. A one-make MINI Challenge race series started in 2004, and a separate series for JCW cars launched four years later. Those JCW Challenge cars could hit 100kmh (0–62mph) in six seconds (and stop in half the time) and hit a 240kmh (149mph) top speed.

Even the original car's rallying success was sort of emulated. A MINI Countryman lookalike won the notoriously demanding Dakar rally four years in succession from 2012–2015. Only the windscreen, lights and door handles were actually carried over from the production Countryman. It rode on massive all-terrain tyres and heavy-duty suspension, featuring double the number of shock absorbers you would find on a road-going car. Power came from a twin-turbo diesel engine borrowed from the BMW 535d, albeit thoroughly re-tuned to cope with desert racing. The body is five per cent larger and incorporates a survival cell, roll cage and space for enough supplies for two people for the two-week, 5,500-mile event. That probably explains why the X-Raid team opted for the larger Countryman instead of the MINI hatchback.

Throughout the 2010s the Dakar rally took place in South America, due to terror threats in Africa (the original route started in Paris, then crossed the Sahara desert to Dakar in Senegal). Since 2020 the rally has been held in Saudi Arabia, and a similar MINI John Cooper Works Buggy has won both the 2020 and 2021 events. Frenchman Stéphane Peterhansel – a certified 14-time Dakar-winning legend – racked up three wins in the MINIs, while Nani Roma, Nasser Al-Attiyah and Carlos Sainz also got the top spot.

BELOW: The modern MINI has continued the brand's proud motorsport heritage, while displaying incredible versatility across a variety of racing disciplines, including the Dakar Rally.

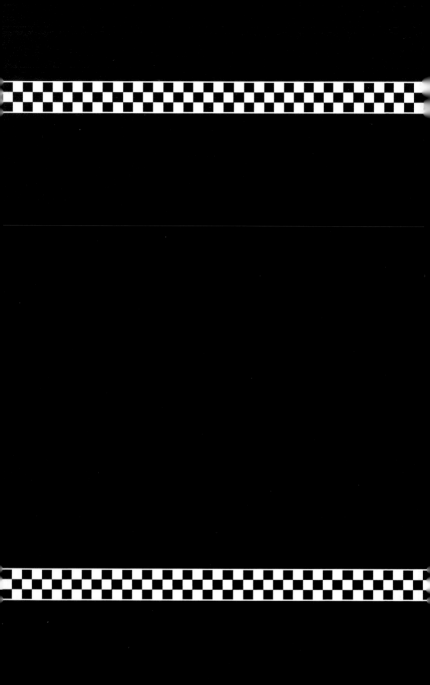

THE MINI
RE-INVENTED

DAWN OF
A NEW ERA

While the 1960s was a decade of The Beatles, James Bond and landing a man on the moon, the new MINI was launched into a time of Britney Spears, the World Wide Web and people just about getting over the fear of microwaves blowing up at the start of a new millennium. Not better or worse – just different – and the modern MINI had to slot into the new decade just as well as the original Mini had lit up the 1960s.

BMW bought out the Rover Group (formerly British Leyland) in 1994, and immediately looked to create the next Mini. The Germans pinched the good bits from Rover Group, and discarded the Rover and MG brands, as they had never really made much money. There was outrage that a German company would be building the new version of a British legend, but BMW mostly understood what made the Mini so special. The German company has done a stellar job with not only the MINI brand but that of Rolls-Royce as well.

Enough context: it's time to see some odd concept cars revealed in the late 1990s. Coming up with a successor to such an iconic car was quite a challenge – like a musician's difficult

OPPOSITE: BMW soon put any lingering doubts as to whether they could live up to the Mini legacy to rest.

ABOVE: The Mini
ACV 30 concept was
rear-wheel-drive
and mid-engined,
because it was based
on the MG F roadster.

second album. That's plain to see with the MINI Spiritual and
Spiritual Too concepts. The Spiritual concept was the same
length as the original Mini, and was equally well packaged,
thanks to wheels that were so far out from the body that they'd
have had a different postcode. It just looked a bit strange, and
rather characterless next to the original, but the BMW Group
boss liked it and called it a decade ahead of its time.

The MINI ACV30 concept was a bit more like it, and
was launched with bonnet stripes, a "floating" roof and an
upturned grille with four spotlamps. While all the cues from
the '60s rally cars were there, it did unfortunately look like a
Mini that's been left out in the sun too long and has melted.
Enthusiasts will point out that it was also rear-wheel drive,
because it was based on the MG F roadster platform, but it was
said to retain the original car's go kart-like handling.

THE NEW MINI

Just a month after the last original Mini left the production line, BMW pulled the wraps off the new one at the 2000 Berlin Motor Show, although it wouldn't go on sale until April 2001. It was bigger in every dimension, giving more space while retaining the proportions of the original – not to mention the front-drive platform and transverse engine. And it had bucketloads of character. A lot of the styling cues had been carried over, but the engines were much more powerful and modern. It was unashamedly retro in style, but buyers loved that; waiting lists were huge and some people paid well over the list price in order to be a trendsetter.

Even the base MINI One got 90hp, 20hp more than the old Cooper S. It was even quite well kitted-out for the cheapest model, with a CD player, electric windows and fog lights. The new MINI Cooper came the following January,

OVERLEAF: MINI loves to riff off its heritage, and often takes inspiration from classic models for its newest versions.

BELOW: The MINI One 7 was one of several special editions that continued the brand's tradition of producing limited-run models.

with a decent 115hp output – more than many similarly sized cars today.

Up until the launch of the MINI, small cars and premium cars were sort of mutually exclusive. Yes, there had been Ghia versions of Ford Fiestas, and the Riley Elf was essentially an upmarket Mini, but the new MINI showed that you didn't have to have a sea of uninspiring black plastic in a supermini. It brought a dash of luxury to buyers who had never been able to afford it before, and appealed to city types who needed something easy to park without giving up on luxurious interior materials.

Famously, Madonna had a black Cooper S from 2002 to 2006, with a whole heap of extras on it... including the

signatures of all the people who assembled it at MINI's Oxford plant. She sang about it in her song 'American Life', and was often papped in the car around London. It last came up for sale in 2018, in pristine condition, with just 25,000 miles on the clock and a seriously chunky £55,000 price tag.

The Cooper S model joined the range six months on from the Cooper, but many had to wait much longer, as demand far exceeded the production line. It was worth the wait. Marked out by a bonnet scoop and twin exhausts, its 1.6-litre engine got an exotic supercharger rather than a more common turbocharger, and was good for 0–100kmh (0–62mph) in around seven seconds with a 217kmh (135mph) top speed. It also received a six-speed manual gearbox, while normal

ABOVE: MINI proudly builds its new cars at a wide-reaching plant in Oxford, before they get exported to the world.

RIGHT: The Rocketman was a concept that was smaller than the standard MINI, as a way of getting closer to the classic Mini. Not a homage to Elton John.

cars were limited to a five-speed one or a less-than-brilliant CVT automatic. A "rocketship" Cooper S Works model was available with around 210hp – an astonishing amount, considering the 2021 Cooper S only has 178hp.

At this stage, the John Cooper Works model was an aftermarket conversion rather than a top-of-the-range version. It had a number of mechanical changes over the Cooper S, but you were denied rear seats and the ability to clean the rear window to save weight. Air conditioning and a radio were not fitted as standard, either, although these could be optioned back in.

At the other end of the scale, a diesel MINI was introduced for the first time in 2003. It too got a six-speed gearbox, but considerably less oomph; 75hp meant hurrying anywhere wasn't really an option. Then again, the Toyota-sourced lump would apparently do 59mpg (268l), so cost about as much as a Freddo to run.

LEFT: Cooper S versions were very quick, with a supercharged engine capable of 0-62mph in 7.4 seconds and a 135mph top speed.

MAKERS OF THE MINI – FRANK STEPHENSON

The man tasked to redesign a classic was Frank Stephenson. He had designed the Ford Escort RS Cosworth and its whaletail spoiler, but the new MINI was one of his greatest hits. He would go on to design the first BMW X5 SUV, the reimagined Fiat 500 and McLaren's new supercar range, plus Ferrari and Maserati racing cars.

Stephenson's pen drew some varied shapes, but then he had not really had a "normal" upbringing. Born in Casablanca, Morocco, he would go on to live in Turkey and Spain, become a professional motocross rider and move to California to study design. He speaks four languages, and since leaving McLaren has branched out into aviation – working on an electric jet capable of vertical take-offs and landings (VTOL).

RIGHT: Celebrated car designer Frank Stephenson was tasked with creating a replacement for the iconic Mini.

THE NEW NEW MINI

ABOVE: A MINI coupé was introduced to appeal to young buyers. Famously, its roof shape was inspired by a backwards baseball cap.

A second-generation MINI was launched in 2006, with bigger fog lights and the reverse lights now in the middle of the tail-light clusters. It looks pretty much identical to the "old" new MINI, yet every single panel was new. The bonnet scoop was in the same place on Cooper S models, but *technically* it was purely for aesthetics as, being turbocharged rather than supercharged, the Cooper S no longer needed the scoop to funnel cool air into the engine.

Diesel cars were really hitting the peak of their popularity in the UK when this generation of the MINI arrived, so buyers had an increasing choice of oil-burners. The One D (nothing to do with One Direction) was joined by Cooper D and Cooper SD models, the latter being a diesel hot hatch promising performance and parsimony in equal measure. Even the mid-range Cooper D would stroll from 0–100kmh (0–62mph) in under 10 seconds, and the promise of 72mpg

BELOW: Released in 2009, the MINI 50 Mayfair and 50 Camden editions celebrated the original car. They were more stylish and luxurious than standard versions.

ABOVE: The MINI
Convertible was
always set to be a
member of the range,
and proved popular
in convertible-keen
Britain.

(4.5l) meant you could enjoy the MINI lifestyle and fill up approximately once a decade. Not that any of those buyers would ever have reached 72mpg (4.5l) given how unrealistic the emissions test was.

The Mini/MINI marked its 50th anniversary in 2009, and that meant one thing: special edition time! You could buy the MINI 50 Mayfair and MINI 50 Camden editions, and a MINI John Cooper Works World Championship 50 version. The first two were available on Cooper, Cooper S and Cooper D models. Mayfair models got extra spotlamps and special badges next to the side repeater indicators, and could be ordered in a fetching brown-on-brown colour scheme. Camden cars rode on exclusive alloys and also featured new badging and darkened headlights.

It wasn't just BMW that celebrated the milestone: the Royal Mail and Royal Mint released commemorative stamps and coins, and 10,000 Mini owners gathered with their pride and joys at Silverstone in May. From August 2009, you could also hitch a ride around London in an original Mini Cooper.

Another limited edition was created to mark the London 2012 Olympic Games, and was then used in the opening ceremony to celebrate Britain. Just don't mention the MINI's German underpinnings. Each of the 2,012 cars built came with an off-centre Union Jack stripe, a few London 2012 logos and an etching of the London skyline on the dashboard.

One final special edition worth mentioning is the Inspired by Goodwood edition, which cost an eye-watering £41,000 – more than double the £18,015 price of the Cooper S. But this was no ordinary MINI; in fact, it was developed in conjunction with Rolls-Royce, and featured leather and walnut veneer, cashmere upholstery and super-thick lambs' wool carpets. Even the paint came from Rolls-Royce.

BELOW: As such an iconic vehicle and a symbol of Britain, it was only right that a Mini appeared in the opening ceremony of the 2012 Olympic Games in London.

OPPOSITE: To
highlight its
Britishness, the MINI
range now comes
with Union Jack-
shaped brake lights.

ANOTHER NEW MINI

The following year, the third-generation BMW-produced MINI hit the road, although not to universal acclaim. It had been made bigger and more rounded, mainly to improve pedestrian safety. It's a far cry from Sir Alec Issigonis' claims that if people got in a crash it was their own fault. Enormous new tail-lights were included to make the MINI look more compact, while sporty versions got chins that Desperate Dan would've been proud of. LED headlamps were available for the first time (in 2021 they are now standard-fit), as you'll know if you've ever been blinded by a MINI coming towards you.

Arguably the styling of the newest MINI has aged pretty well, and a stream of subtle updates have kept it looking fresh. Post-2016 cars get tail-lights inspired by the British Union Jack flag, for example.

Optional extras have always been a big part of the MINI experience, with near-endless packs and graphics to make your car stand out from the crowd. The brand itself says that it's incredibly unlikely that two absolutely identical MINIs will leave the factory in the same year. Just on the roof alone, it has been possible to choose things like chequered flag graphics, the MINI logo, a range of contrasting colours and now a multitone roof that merges from blue to black.

In fact, up until recently it was possible to *double* the price of a base-spec MINI One with optional extras, if you wanted a fully stocked MINI with very little power.

It's a long way from the original Mini, which was sparsely equipped to the point that it didn't offer even a heater or a radio. Now, every MINI leaves the factory with automatic headlights, digital radio, a touchscreen and a system that will automatically contact the emergency services if you have a crash.

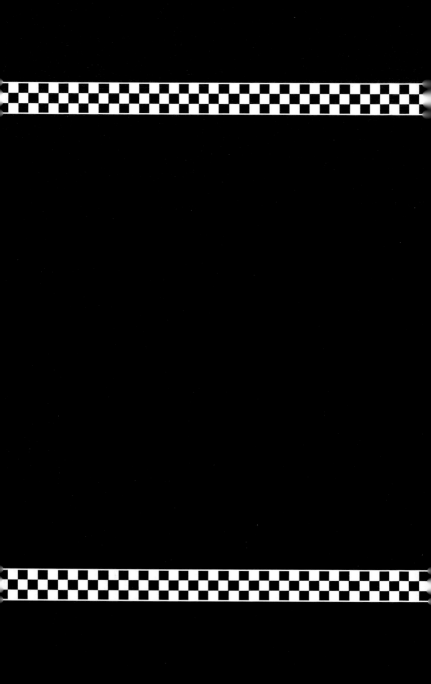

A MINI MONEYSPINNER

THE FUTURE IS BRIGHT

At the time of writing this book, the new MINI is currently celebrating its 20th anniversary. In that time we've gone from CD Walkmans and the first-ever mobile phone to have a colour display, to smartphones that render most other devices redundant. The MINI hatchback has changed and adapted to flow with the times, but it has not been the only MINI-badged car to launch in that time.

BMW saw money-making branding opportunities with the MINI name, and it has broadened the range with a glut of new models. The partnership has arguably strengthened both brands, as development was shared across the companies – so the MINIs got BMW's luxury materials and BMW could engineer front-wheel drive models when they had almost exclusively been known for rear-drive cars previously.

OPPOSITE: The most hardcore MINI ever is the third-generation John Cooper Works GP model, with carbon-fibre skirts and a limited production run.

RIGHT: You can open the MINI Convertible's roof at up to 18mph, and doing so takes just 15 seconds.

MINI CONVERTIBLE

Hacking the roof off the hatchback gave buyers an open-roofed MINI Convertible option in 2004, and sun-seeking British buyers absolutely lapped it up. Fashionable and trendy, 164,000 units were sold in the first four years, in One, Cooper and Cooper S versions with between 90 and 170hp. The roof came up and down at the touch of a button, so in 15 seconds you could switch from privacy to everyone seeing you. When down, the roof sat proudly on the top of the back end – and still does now.

This wasn't actually the first drop-top Mini. An aftermarket company produced a few in 1991, and Rover liked this wobbly lettuce leaf of a car so much that it bought the tooling and started making an official version. If you have never seen one, it's because only 1,000 were sold between 1993 and 1996.

The BMW-built MINI Convertible had a drop-down tailgate like the original Mini, and the boot lid could hold up to 80kg (176lb), so it could be used as extra luggage space (if the thing you were carrying was strapped down). The folding roof meant there was not a lot of room for your stuff, nor the people sitting in the rear seats, and with the roof down you could see almost nothing out of the rear-view mirror. Not that that bothered many buyers, of course.

The supercharged Cooper S convertible was a surprise, but an even faster model came with the second-generation new MINI. A John Cooper Works version with 211hp meant you could go from straight to curly hair in just 6.9 seconds, and on to a 235kmh (146mph) top speed. The 2021 edition is faster still, and a little more economical, but crashes into potholes and never really gets comfortable. All 2021 Convertibles now feature a Union Jack roof as standard, so you had better buy into the Britishness.

MINI CLUBMAN

Two became three in autumn 2007, with the new MINI Clubman model. It brought back the classic Clubman name, but this time around for an estate model – so it's the modern-day Austin Countryman or Mini Traveller. The Clubman had an extra eight centimetres (3in) between the front and rear wheels, and barn doors like the classic versions. It still wasn't particularly practical, but it wasn't meant to be a boring, well-packaged estate car.

Curiously, the Clubman also came with an extra door on the right-hand side, but not on the left. The extra door meant access to the spacious rear seats was much easier, but it was designed for left-hand-drive markets (Germany in particular) – and the fuel filler was located on the other side. Parallel-park

BELOW: A new MINI Clubman launched in 2007. It proved slightly divisive at the time, and the rear door was said to be on the 'wrong' side of the car for UK buyers.

in the UK and your rear-seat passengers will be getting out into the road, rather than onto the pavement. The motoring press weren't too kind about its looks when it launched – and mocked the silly doors – but nowadays it has aged quite well.

The Clubman led to the Clubvan, which pretended to be a commercial vehicle by getting rid of the rear seats and rear windows. It made sense to some small businesses, and was cheaper than the Clubman because you didn't need to pay VAT, due to it being classed as a van. You'll occasionally see one in the UK, but only 50 were sold in the US, where it was costlier than the Clubman.

A replacement MINI Clubman launched in 2015, and look – a rear door on each side...! But still two barn doors on the back, making it the only six-door car that is not a limousine or a funeral car. It was available for the first time with a new eight-speed automatic gearbox and MINI's All4 four-wheel-drive system. Top of the range is the John Cooper Works version which, from August 2019, gets a huge 306hp and the ability to crack 0–100kmh (0–62mph) in under five seconds.

MINI COUNTRYMAN SUV

If you need proof of the MINI's trendiness, the first MINI Countryman crossover came at a time when SUVs were starting to be real hot stuff for car buyers. The 2010 Countryman was a model that you could actually use as a family car, as it had four passenger doors and a proper tailgate – and space within. It used most of the same styling features as the MINI, making it recognizably related to the hatchback, but on a bigger scale.

The original Countryman was previewed by the MINI Beachcomber concept, which eschewed doors for an open, carefree feel. It had the All4 system and chunky off-road tyres, but never made it to production due to MINI's concerns about the safety of going door-less.

OVERLEAF: MINI paid homage to the Mini Moke with the Beachcomber concept. It previewed the Countryman and was a bit better equipped than the Moke – even coming with an MP3 player and a cool box.

BELOW: The Countryman name was reintroduced for the brand's first crossover, which was available with four-wheel drive and had more space than other MINI models.

A new Countryman launched in late 2016 and it stretched the definition of "mini" even more, being 20cm (8in) longer than the model it replaced. New styling updates mean it looks even chunkier and rugged than the first-generation model, while the brand's first-ever plug-in hybrid (PHEV) model was introduced as well.

The plug-in hybrid uses the 1.5-litre, 134hp petrol engine from Cooper models, alongside an electric motor and a small battery. It's a similar, if less powerful, setup to the BMW i8 sports car. The hybrid is the second-quickest Countryman, behind the John Cooper Works version, yet it's by far the cleanest and greenest. With the battery fully charged, it's possible to drive 40–48km (25–30) miles on electric power alone, and you can choose how and when the car uses its two forms of power.

MINI PACEMAN, COUPÉ AND ROADSTER

In 2012 MINI decided that what the world needed was a three-door coupé version of the Countryman with a lower roof. The world saw the MINI Paceman and gave it the seal of disapproval. It was unclear where it fitted in the range, and why it was on sale in the first place. Besides the PHEV, all other engines were carried over, but the Paceman only lasted until 2016 before it was withdrawn.

Some of MINI's diversification attempts have gone well (after the Countryman's release it made up a third of MINI's sales in America), some not so well. The Coupé and Roadster were two-seat MINIs, with a hardtop and folding fabric roof respectively. An odd-looking hardtop roof, perhaps, but then MINI's design director at the time, Gert Hildebrand, was inspired by seeing a baseball cap worn backwards. The Roadster, meanwhile, didn't replace the four-seat Convertible, so for three years you could buy two impractical drop-top MINIs, but one was just more impractical than the other. Both the Coupe and Roadster were axed in 2015

ABOVE: MINI also produced a three-door version of the Countryman, called the Paceman.

MINI 5-DOOR

Buyers had already proved that a more spacious MINI would sell well, so the first-ever MINI 5-door hatch was launched in 2014. It brought most of the 3-door's cute looks, but made it doubly easy for your rear-seat passengers to get in and out. Once in, they had a bit more space to enjoy, too. The 5-door has proved more successful than the Paceman and the Coupé, and remains an integral part of the current MINI range.

MINI ELECTRIC

The Countryman hybrid has given buyers a stepping stone to electrification, while buyers who never want to visit a petrol station again can now opt for the MINI Electric. A trial of 130 cars was launched way back in 2009, but now anyone can buy a MINI Electric if they desire. Not only is the Electric just as stylish as any other MINI, it's quick – so you could legitimately choose it over the petrol-powered Cooper S – and can be driven using just the accelerator, as the car slows down as soon as you lift your foot off the pedal.

Besides a fared-in grille and exclusive wheel designs (including a snazzy set that look like UK plug sockets), the Electric looks pretty much like any other MINI. All the electric bits are stashed under the bonnet and the floor, so it's the same inside too. It manages up to 233km (145 miles) between charges; not an awful lot, but a motorway fast-charger will top up the battery to 80 per cent charge in around half an hour – and even a full recharge at home only takes around three hours, while costing much less than a tank of fuel.

OPPOSITE AND BELOW: An electric MINI was introduced for the first time in 2020, giving fans a zero-emission model to choose alongside the petrol versions.

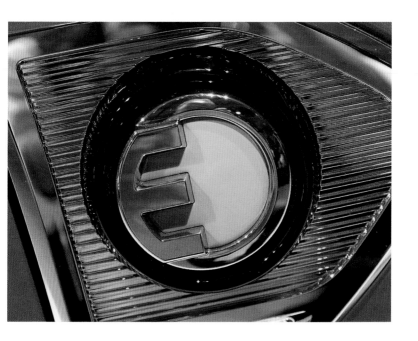

LEFT: The MINI Superleggera concept was built to look pretty at the Villa d'Este luxury car festival. It looks very cool, though, and Superleggera means super-light – the car used lots of innovative materials and techniques to save weight.

MINI JCW GP

Perhaps you want your MINI to be the hardest, fastest and meanest car on the road instead? For years, that has been the John Cooper Works models, which have been available on all the variations mentioned above. All brought super-firm suspension, pumped-up styling and loud exhausts, while the JCW team has always gone one further on MINI hatch models. Each generation of MINI hatch has boasted

a JCW GP version, with a limited production run and just the two seats.

The latest one boasts 306hp – an awful lot for such a small car – and a staggering top speed of 264kmh (164mph). It also brings a whopping rear spoiler and carbon-fibre wheel arch extensions, so it even looks faster than any MINI that came before it. To get the most out of it and use it to its full potential, take it to a racetrack and blast around.

BELOW: A 2020 John Cooper Works GP MINI, with some delicious red detailing, on display in Brussels

MINIS IN THE FUTURE

MINI will be going fully electric by 2030, in line with the UK government's currently proposed ban on sales of new petrol and diesel cars. The last new petrol model will be launched in 2025. A new Countryman is set to launch in 2023 with petrol and fully electric options (no plug-in hybrid next time around), while the MINI hatch will get smaller and there will be a new crossover in the middle. The new one looks set to replace the Clubman estate, and the Convertible may be discontinued as well. I believe a new MINI Convertible is coming, so could we change it to "…Clubman estate, although the Convertible is likely to continue.

The Mini story has continued for over 60 years, and the brand looks in rude health and likely to continue on for a long time to come. Created as an affordable car for the masses, the Mini has survived poor ownership, early reliability problems and much newer competition to become a true icon and a glorious symbol of Britain. It's perhaps the ultimate small car, and has enjoyed one of the longest production runs of all time.

The classic Mini may even be usurped by the new one – in terms of sales, at least. Over its first 41 years, nearly 5.4 million Minis were sold, but by 2019 that number had risen to ten million. That means 4.6 million cars were sold in just 18 years from the new MINI's launch in 2001 and, fittingly, the 10 millionth car was a 60 Years Anniversary Edition. MINI's Plant Oxford factory produces roughly 1,000 cars a day, so the new car is quickly approaching the total of the original classic. Who knows what we'll be driving in another 60 years, but chances are there'll be a Mini that's up for the job.

OPPOSITE: The transition to electric marks the start of another era in the history of MINI, but all signs point to it being a great success.

INDEX

CREDITS

The publishers would like to thank the following sources for their kind permission to reproduce the pictures in this book.

THE ADVERTISING ARCHIVES: 57

ALAMY: /Cavan Images: 155; /culture-images GmbH: 119, 142; / imageBROKER: 144-145; /Motoring Picture Library: 19; /Matthew Richardson: 116; /Mark Scheuern: 126-127; Ian Shipley Auto: 46-47; /TCD/ Prod.DB: 90

BMW GROUP: 4, 8, 16-17, 21, 23, 36-37, 38, 50-51, 52, 54-55, 60, 109, 120-121, 122-123, 130-131, 138

GETTY IMAGES: /Matthew Ashton: 133; /Bettmann: 30-31; /John Drysdale/ Hulton Archive: 33, 49; /Valentin Flauraud/Bloomberg: 128; /Isa Foltin: 91; / Fotografica Inc.: 147; /Fox Photos: 63; /GP Library/Universal Images Group: 69; /Sean Gallup: 149; /Aubrey Hart/Evening Standard: 26; /Keystone-France/ Gamma-Keystone: 42, 67, 78; /Mirrorpix: 39; /NYCshooter: 84-85; /National Motor Museum/Heritage Images: 12-13, 18, 44, 45, 56, 66, 86, 129, 132, 140-141; /Popperfoto: 20, 29; /Jacopo Raule: 124-125; /Oli Scarff: 81; /Science & Society Picture Library: 34; /Silver Screen Collection: 10; /Ted Soqui/Corbis: 150-151; /Tramino: 146; /Sjoerd van der Wal: 135, 148, 152-153; /Western Mail Archive/Mirrorpix: 35; /Wilson/Mirrorpix: 82-83

MOTORSPORT IMAGES: /Jeff Bloxham/LAT: 74-75; /LAT: 15, 94, 96-97, 98-99, 101, 102, 104-105, 106-107, 108; /Sutton Images: 73, 110, 111

SHUTTERSTOCK: 70; /Rodrigo Garrido: 113; /Paul Greaves: 89; /Magic Car Pics: 64-65, 118

Every effort has been made to acknowledge correctly and contact the source and/or copyright holder of each picture any unintentional errors or omissions will be corrected in future editions of this book.